MAINE

Past and Present

Judy Monroe Peterson

rosen publishing's
rosen central®

New York

To Morgan, Ryan, Abbie, Jenna, Jennifer, and Tom, residents of Boothbay Harbor

Published in 2011 by The Rosen Publishing Group, Inc.
29 East 21st Street, New York, NY 10010

Library of Congress Cataloging-in-Publication Data

Peterson, Judy Monroe.
Maine: past and present / Judy Monroe Peterson.
   p. cm. — (The United States: past and present)
Includes bibliographical references and index.
ISBN 978-1-4358-9484-6 (library binding)
ISBN 978-1-4358-9511-9 (pbk.)
ISBN 978-1-4358-9545-4 (6-pack)
1. Maine—Juvenile literature. 2. Maine—History—Juvenile literature. I. Title.
F19.3.P477 2011
974.1—dc22

2009048769

Manufactured in Malaysia

CPSIA Compliance Information: Batch #S10YA: For further information, contact Rosen Publishing, New York, New York, at 1-800-237-9932.

On the cover: Top left: Around 1930, Maine loggers used the Machias River to float logs to lumber mills. Top right: The *Mason*, a U.S. Navy ship, was built at the Bath Iron Works and was launched on the Kennebec River. Bottom: Pemaquid Point Lighthouse near Bristol, Maine, offers a panoramic view of the Atlantic Ocean.

Contents

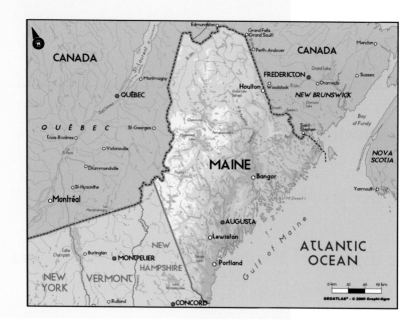

Maine is located in the extreme northeast corner of the United States. It is bordered by New Hampshire, Canada, the Atlantic Ocean, and the Bay of Fundy.

Introduction

More than four hundred years ago, explorers from France sailed along the coast of Maine. They met the resident Native Americans and sent back reports of thick forests and abundant fish along the coastline. Colonists from England arrived next. They were impressed with the natural resources of the area and began to fish, farm, and cut the tall trees for lumber to build ships, villages, and towns.

The people of Maine continue to rely on the many natural resources of the area. The seacoast still provides great numbers of fish and seafood. Inland, people farm and grow crops including blueberries and potatoes. People use wood from the forests to make lumber and paper products.

Maine is a popular place for tourists. The state is known for its beautiful shore along the Atlantic Ocean. Lighthouses, sandy beaches, and fishing villages can be found along the rocky coast. People who like to explore can visit thousands of nearby islands. Many people vacation in Maine to enjoy the lakes, rivers, and mountains and stay at resorts and cabins.

Maine has grown to a population of more than 1.3 million people. Small farms once dotted the state, but large, modern farms have replaced them. However, some things remain the same. Most of the state is still covered with trees. Almost 18 million acres (7 million hectares) of forest cover most of Maine, which is the most heavily forested state in the country. Fishing still provides a livelihood for many people.

Chapter 1

THE GEOGRAPHY OF MAINE

On a map, Maine is located in the northeastern corner of the United States. Its neighbor to the southwest is New Hampshire. The Canadian provinces of New Brunswick and Quebec are its other neighbors to the west, north, and east. The Atlantic Ocean along Maine's coast washes the land for approximately 3,478 miles (5,600 kilometers). The coastline of Maine has many deep harbors, jagged rocks and cliffs, sandy beaches, and thousands of bays, coves, and inlets.

Maine is in New England, a region made up of five other states: Connecticut, Massachusetts, New Hampshire, Rhode Island, and Vermont. Maine measures 35,385 square miles (91,647 sq km) in total area. All of the other New England states combined could nearly fit inside Maine.

Islands of Maine

More than two thousand islands dot Maine's waters. The largest island is Mount Desert Island. It measures 100 square miles (260 sq km). Much of this island of forests and mountains is protected as Acadia National Park, the only national park in New England. Cadillac Mountain rises 1,530 feet (466 meters) on Mount Desert Island. It is the highest point on the Atlantic coast in North America.

Built in 1858, Bass Harbor Head Lighthouse, located near Acadia National Park, ranks as one of the most-photographed lighthouses in New England. It is on the southern tip of Mount Desert Island.

People do not live on most of the islands. Some islands, though, are part of cities, such as islands in Casco Bay located on the southern coast of Maine. People who live on these beautiful islands take ferries to get to Portland, Maine's largest city.

The Three Regions of Maine

Maine has three natural geographic areas. They are the Coastal Lowlands, the Eastern New England Upland, and the White Mountains Region.

The Coastal Lowlands cover southeastern Maine. They belong to an area in New England also called the Coastal Lowlands. The

The Puffins of Maine

The colorful Atlantic puffin was once abundant along the coast of Maine. The state was the only place in the United States where the small seabirds lived. Most make their home along the far north Atlantic coastline. Also called the sea parrot or clown of the ocean, Atlantic puffins measure about 10 inches (18 centimeters) long. They have a black back, bright white chest and cheeks, and orange legs. Their large, triangular beak is red, yellow, and blue. Puffins live in colonies and build nests on coastal land. Excellent divers and underwater swimmers, they eat small fish.

The birds were nearly wiped out in Maine. Early settlers ate them and their eggs. Rats arriving on ships also ate their eggs. The birds were killed for their feathers, which were used to decorate hats. The fish that puffins ate become scarce because of large-scale fishing operations. By 1900, only two small colonies of puffins remained in the Gulf of Maine.

In 1973, Stephen W. Kress, a Maine ornithologist (a person who studies birds), started Project Puffin. He wanted to bring the seabirds back to Eastern Egg Rock Island. He brought nearly one thousand puffin chicks from a large colony in Canada and raised them on the island. He hoped the adult birds would return to Eastern Egg Rock and raise their chicks. The first puffins returned in 1977, and more followed. A similar plan was used at Seal Island National Wildlife Refuge, with puffins returning in 1992. Currently, the Atlantic puffins make their home on five Maine islands.

Today, about fourteen million Atlantic puffins are found from Maine to Norway. Most of their lives are spent at sea. When diving for fish, puffins usually stay underwater for thirty seconds or less. However, they can dive 200 feet (61 m) deep and stay down for up to sixty seconds. In the air, they can fly at 55 miles per hour (88 meters per hour).

narrow strip of lowland winds along the entire coast of New England. In Maine, this region is about 10 to 20 miles (16 to 32 km) inland from the Atlantic Ocean. Sandy beaches blanket the coast in the south of Maine. Near Portland is Old Orchard Beach. This smooth, sandy beach is one of the largest on the Atlantic coast, and many tourists visit there. West of the beaches are salt marshes. Bands of sand or bays between high cliffs cover the northeast coastal area.

Maine ranks fifth in the nation for potato production. Most of the state's crop comes from farms in Aroostook County.

Northwest of the Coastal Lowlands lies the Eastern New England Upland. This region stretches from the border of Canada to Connecticut. The Uplands of Maine is the state's largest area. It measures 20 to 50 miles (32 to 80 km) wide. In the east, the land rises from near sea level to about 2,000 feet (610 meters) in the west. The Aroostook Plateau is in the far northeast of the Uplands. Farmers raise crops in the rich soil. South of the plateau are many lakes and streams. Rugged mountains cut through the center of the Uplands.

Northwestern Maine contains the White Mountains Region. These rugged mountains also cover part of New Hampshire and Vermont. In Maine, the White Mountains Region is about 5 miles (8 km) wide in the north and spreads to 30 miles (48 km) wide in the south. The White Mountains Region includes hundreds of lakes and most of Maine's highest mountains. At 5,267 feet (1,606 m), Mount

Katahdin towers as the tallest peak in Maine. More than one hundred other mountains measure more than 3,000 feet (910 m) high.

Rivers and Lakes

In addition to the coastline along the Atlantic Ocean, the state has more than five thousand freshwater rivers and streams. The St. John is the longest river in northern Maine. Large power plants along the river use the moving water to create electricity. Two other important rivers, the Kennebec and the Penobscot, wind down the center of the state and empty into the ocean. The Androscoggin River and the Saco River flow across southern Maine and spill into the ocean.

Moosehead Lake is Maine's largest lake. The lake, measuring 120 square miles (311 sq km), is located in the west-central part of the state.

Plants and Animals

Forests cover nearly 90 percent of Maine and are made up of mostly softwood trees, including fir, pine, and spruce. Important hardwood trees are basswood, beech, maple, oak, and white and yellow birch. Hundreds of varieties of flowering plants grow in Maine, including wild blueberries, seventeen rare types of orchid, and many wildflowers.

Birdwatchers can count more than 320 kinds of birds in Maine, including loons, duck, geese, blue herons, egrets, owls, falcons, eagles, and ospreys. More than twenty thousand large moose range throughout Maine. The state is also home to many black bears, white-tailed deer, beavers, and porcupines. Other abundant animals include fishers, marten, coyotes, red foxes, rabbits, and squirrels.

Moose live in thick forests near shallow water. The lakes, marshes, and swamps provide a source of food. Moose are excellent swimmers and can run fast.

Maine's lakes and streams contain freshwater fish including brook trout, salmon, smallmouth bass, and perch. All are good to eat. Tasty ocean fish caught along the coast include cod, flounder, mackerel, pollock, striped bass, and tuna. Humpback, right, finback, and minke whales can be found in the coastal waters. One can also spot harbor porpoises traveling in groups and huge basking sharks and giant ocean sunfish. Playful harbor seals swim in most harbors along the coast.

Climate

Because the ocean tempers the climate in Maine, summers are cool, ranging from 60 to 80 degrees Fahrenheit (15 to 27 degrees Celsius). Winter temperatures range from 20 to 40°F (-7 to 4°C).

Chapter 2

THE HISTORY OF MAINE

Maine's history began about ten thousand years ago. At that time, thousands of Native Americans lived along the Penobscot River in what is now Maine. They belonged to the Abenaki and Etchemin tribes of the Algonquian group of Native Americans. Although they built villages, they often moved to hunt, fish, and gather berries and nuts.

Exploration and Settlements

England sent explorers John Cabot and his son, Sebastian, to the coast of Maine. They arrived in 1497 and claimed the New England region for England. France also sent explorers to Maine, including Giovanni da Verrazano, who arrived in 1524. Verrazano claimed the region for France. The first French colony in Maine was founded by Samuel de Champlain and Pierre du Gua, Sieur (Lord) de Monts, in 1604. The French colony was abandoned after a hard winter.

In 1605, English explorer George Waymouth sailed along the Maine coast. He returned to England, reporting on the tall, thick forests and abundant wildlife and fish. As a result, in 1607, a group of English colonists started the Popham Colony near the mouth of the Kennebec River. After many hardships, they sailed back to England

This painting depicts John and Sebastian Cabot leaving Bristol, England, in 1497. That same year, the explorers arrived in Maine and claimed the land for England.

a year later. By the early 1620s, other English colonists had made many settlements in the region.

Ferdinando Gorges established Maine's first government in 1636. In 1641, he made the community of Gorgeana (now York) a city. It was the first chartered English city in what is now the United States. Ten years later, Maine became part of the Massachusetts Bay Colony, governed by Great Britain.

Maine's population increased over the next century. The colonists used the natural resources of the region. They cut trees for timber and shipbuilding. Many small farms sprang up.

The Flags of Maine

Until 1820, Maine was part of Massachusetts, and its flags were based on that connection. Most early flags were associated with the military of Massachusetts. Until the Civil War, Maine's flag was blue with the state's coat of arms. The coat of arms displayed a pine tree used in the naval flag of Massachusetts since April 1776. The shipbuilding industry of northern New England was based on its pine trees.

A law for Maine's first official flag passed on March 21, 1901. This flag had a light tan background with a pine tree in the center and a blue star. The star represented the North Star, a symbol of Maine as the most northern state in the United States in 1820. The North Star was also important to help guide sailors' ships at sea.

A new law was passed on February 23, 1909, which greatly changed the state flag. Now the flag had a blue background, with the Maine coat of arms displayed on a shield. The coat of arms shows a pine tree, a moose, land with trees, and the sea.

Today, variations of the state flag are used. Because no official colors for the arms exist, the color of the forest scene on the shield can differ. The model of the state flag displays purple trees behind the white pine tree. Other flags have the trees as red, orange, pink, yellow, or green. In addition, Maine is one of only two states with a merchant marine flag that ships and boats use. This flag has a white background and a green pine tree in the center. Above the tree is the state motto in Latin, *Dirigo* (which means "I lead"). Below the tree is the state name, Maine, and behind is an anchor on its side. Both the state name and anchor are colored blue.

The Revolutionary War

During the 1760s, Great Britain passed a series of laws on the colonies. The colonists paid heavy taxes and followed laws restricting their trade. In protest, a group of Maine colonists burned a cargo of British tea stored at York in 1774. The York Tea Party was based on the famous Boston Tea Party of 1773.

The Revolutionary War (1775–1783) started at Lexington and Concord, Massachusetts. Hundreds of Maine colonists fought for independence from England. Angry British troops burned Falmouth (now Portland) to punish the townspeople. The first naval battle of the Revolutionary War was fought off Machias, Maine, in June 1775. In the battle, Maine patriots captured the British ship *Margaretta*.

Statehood and the Civil War

When the Revolutionary War ended in 1783, the thirteen colonies had become a new nation, the United States of America. Although still part of Massachusetts, people in Maine wanted to form their own state and be admitted to the Union. Maine prepared for statehood by writing its first constitution. It was adopted in December 1819, about three months before Maine became a state. Maine applied for statehood in 1819 and became the twenty-third state on March 15, 1820. Portland was chosen as the capital. In 1832, the capital moved to Augusta because of its central location.

Maine's admission was part of the Missouri Compromise. In Maine, slavery had always been illegal. The plan called for Maine to enter as a free state and Missouri to enter as a slave state. This arrangement kept the number of slave and free states equal.

Tensions within the country over slavery led to the Civil War in 1861. About seventy-two thousand Maine men joined the Union forces during the American Civil War and fought for the Union, which won the war in 1865. During the war, Hannibal Hamlin, a former U.S. senator and governor of Maine, served as vice president of the United States under President Abraham Lincoln.

Hannibal Hamlin (*right*) is pictured here in a campaign button with Abraham Lincoln. Hamlin served as U.S. vice president under President Lincoln from 1860 to 1861.

Taking Care of Maine's Environment

During the 1890s, Maine began developing hydroelectric power along its rivers. Plentiful electricity helped fuel Maine's industrial growth. The state soon became a leader in the shipbuilding, textile, and papermaking industries. New industries came to Maine in the 1950s and 1960s, including food packaging and electronics manufacturing. Large commercial farms replaced small family farms.

Today, Maine faces many environmental issues. Factory and agricultural waste has spilled into lakes, rivers, and streams and along the coastline. As a result, many freshwater and sea animals have been killed, and some water has become unsafe to drink. People concerned about clean water have helped pass laws that have forced factories, cities, and towns to improve their waste removal.

Lake Katahdin can be seen from the top of Mount Katahdin. Maine is the most heavily forested state in the nation. The public owns only about 6 percent of the state's forests—the rest are held by private landowners.

Other natural resources have been damaged. Overfishing has reduced yields from the Atlantic Ocean. Loggers have cut many of Maine's valuable trees. Tree farms have helped to protect the forests, but overcutting of trees is still an issue.

Laws have been passed to address overharvesting of timber, water pollution, and developing wilderness areas. Government, communities, and individuals have worked together to protect Maine's environment. Preserving and using the state's natural resources will continue to be a challenge.

Chapter 3

THE GOVERNMENT OF MAINE

Maine is governed under its original constitution. The constitution of Maine divides the state government into three branches: the executive, legislative, and judicial. Although each branch has its own special functions, they all work together to help run the state. Each branch of government balances the other two, so one branch cannot get too much power.

Any amendment to the constitution must be proposed by a two-thirds vote in the state legislature. To make an amendment into law, a majority of the state's voters must vote for it in a regular election. In addition, an amendment can be proposed by a constitutional convention. A two-thirds vote in the legislature is needed to call a constitutional convention.

Maine elects two representatives and two senators to the U.S. Congress. The state has four electoral votes in the electoral college for presidential elections.

The Executive Branch

The executive branch carries out the laws of the state. The governor heads this branch and makes decisions with the help of a cabinet of experts on major public issues, such as the state's economy, taxes, and education. The public elects the governor every four years. A governor can serve only two consecutive four-year terms but has no limit on the number of terms served. The governor has offices on the second floor of the State House in Augusta.

The responsibilities of the governor include approving or vetoing bills passed by the legislature and setting the state budget. The governor appoints other department heads in the executive branch, including heads of agriculture, conservation, education, public safety, and more.

The governor of Maine lives in the governor's mansion, also called Blaine House. In 1919, the mansion was given to the state.

Other constitutional officials in the executive branch are the secretary of state, the attorney general, and the state treasurer. These officials are members of the governor's cabinet. The legislature elects each of these officials for two-year terms. The state auditor serves a four-year term and is elected by the legislature. The state auditor studies the state's financial records and makes a report to the legislature every year.

The Legislative Branch

The legislative branch makes, passes, and repeals state laws and approves the state budget. Like the federal government, Maine's legislature is made up of two houses, or parts: the state senate and the

Soon after Augusta became the official capital of Maine in 1827, work began on the Maine State House. Built using Maine granite, the capitol building was completed in 1832.

house of representatives. Both houses meet every year in the State House in Augusta for two sessions, beginning in January.

The state senate consists of 35 members, and the house of representatives has 151 members. A member of the legislature is called a legislator. A legislator is elected by the public for a term of two years. A 1993 law limits the number of consecutive terms a legislator can serve to four.

The Judicial Branch

The judicial branch hears legal cases and interprets and enforces state laws. It has three levels of courts: district and probate courts, superior court, and supreme judicial court. Maine's thirty-one district courts are spread out among the state's thirteen districts. The district courts hear cases involving damages of less than $20,000. They handle divorces, juvenile offenders, and minor criminal and civil cases, such as traffic tickets or trespassing. District court judges serve seven-year terms. Probate courts deal with adoptions, wills, and estates.

The next highest court is the superior court. This court handles all cases requiring trial by jury and all cases appealed from lower courts. The fourteen superior court justices serve seven-year terms.

The Maine Supreme Court is the highest, or most powerful, court in the state. It hears cases that are appealed from lower courts. The supreme court has a chief justice (judge) and six associate justices. All serve for a seven-year term. The chief justice heads the judicial branch.

The governor nominates all justices of the supreme, superior, and district courts. They are appointed with two-thirds of the senate approval. All judges except for probate judges serve full-time. Probate judges serve part-time and are elected by the voters of each county for four-year terms.

Local Government

In Maine, local government provides many essential services to the community. These services include roads, parks, disposal of solid waste, public utilities, waste water treatment, police, fire protection, and public education for kindergarten through high school.

On the local level, Maine has 16 counties, 22 cities, and 433 towns. Every county has its own government. Each city has home rule, or self-government in local matters. The cities typically have a mayor-council or city-manager form of government.

Most towns are made up of several communities governed together as a unit. The annual town meeting is the most common form of government in Maine towns. This New England tradition allows people to take a direct part in government. At town meetings, citizens can discuss their concerns, make suggestions, and vote on issues. An elective board supervises town affairs between meetings.

Maine's Courts

Maine did not have its own court system before 1820. Instead, its courts were part of the Massachusetts court system. After Maine joined the Union, its new constitution went into effect. Article Six of the Maine Constitution established the judicial branch of government: "The judicial power of the State be vested in a Supreme Judicial Court, and such other courts as the Legislature shall from time to time establish." The supreme judicial court could hear civil or criminal cases and review decisions of lower courts. The legislature created the county-based probate courts that same year.

The Court Reorganization Act of 1852 added to the power of the supreme judicial court. Now the court could hear almost all types of case. The number of justices was increased, and they could travel in circuits (several different places within a judicial district) to hear cases. By the 1920s, the supreme judicial court had too much work. As a result, in 1929, the legislature created the statewide superior court to decrease the workload of the supreme judicial court.

The next big change to Maine's courts came in 1961. The state ended the municipal courts and the trial justices system. A new statewide district court with thirty-six judges was created. As a result, Maine's court system became one of the most unified in the nation. Now all courts, except the probate system, were under state management. During the 1990s, specialized divisions were created within the Maine court system. Some of the divisions included the Family Division of the Maine District Court, the Juvenile Drug Treatment Court Program, and the Adult Drug Court Program. On January 1, 2001, the state legislature further unified Maine's courts. The district court became the only court to handle divorce and family cases. In addition, appeals could now be filed to law court from district court. The workload of the superior court was eased with these changes. Today, Maine's court systems continue to work well for its people.

The chief town officials are called selectmen.

Another unit of local government in Maine is the plantation. Each of the thirty-four plantations has a limited form of self-government. A plantation is governed by a board of assessors. Plantations are usually found in areas with small, usually rural, populations.

These people are singing the national anthem before their annual town meeting in Rome, Maine. During town meetings, citizens pass laws, adopt a budget, and elect the selectmen and other town officials.

The 422 townships in Maine have no organized government. The townships are grouped into thirty-six territories. In addition, the state has three self-governing Native American townships. Each is headed by a governor, a lieutenant governor, and a tribal council.

Chapter 4

THE ECONOMY OF MAINE

During its first hundred years, Maine's economy was based on fishing, trading, and products from its vast forests. Until the late 1700s, the white pine tree was the main resource of Maine. Most of these large trees were used to make masts for wooden ships. New industries, such as textile mills and shoe factories, came to Maine during the 1830s to 1860s. Many of these factories later moved to the South because costs for materials and labor were lower. In addition, ships made from steel and iron were quickly replacing wooden ships. After the Civil War (1861–1865), Maine's forests became important for supplying a new and growing paper industry.

Today, ports along the coast provide a base for Maine's fishing and shipbuilding industries. Lumber and wood-processing industries are an important part of the state's economy. Other manufacturing industries such as mining contribute to the economy, as well as newer industries like biotechnology and electronics. Agriculture and food processing employ many people. The natural beauty of the state attracts millions of tourists every year. The service industry, which includes tourism, is now the largest part of the state's economy.

In 2009, Maine's total value of goods and services produced (gross domestic product, or GDP) was $50.0 billion. As of 2009, nearly 664,800 people had jobs in the state.

Workers stack logs at a lumber company in Piscataquis County. Much of Maine's rural timber industry has shut down, cut back, or changed hands.

Manufacturing Industry

In the 1960s, manufacturing made up about half of the jobs in Maine. By 2009, manufacturing jobs had fallen to 14 percent. Currently, forest-based products made in factories include cardboard boxes, paper bags, furniture, matches, clothespins, and toothpicks. Maine is the nation's leader in making toothpicks and the second leading producer of paper. Many cities have pulp and paper mills to manufacture these products. However, people continue to lose their jobs in the mills due to increased automation.

Other manufactured items made in the state are transportation equipment for boats and ships and plastics. The making of computer,

PAST AND PRESENT

The Wild Blueberries of Maine

Wild blueberries are native to Maine, eastern Canada, and other scattered areas in the northern United States. They are smaller and more flavorful than the kind grown on farms. The fruit was a survival food for the early Native Americans. They ate them fresh or dried. They taught European settlers how to pick and dry wild blueberries in the sun for use all year. The Native Americans also showed the colonists how to burn areas of pine forests to encourage the growth of wild blueberries. The plant grew well where there were pine trees because of the acidic soil.

Maine's wild blueberries were first harvested for sale in the 1840s. Fresh wild blueberries were brought to other states by train. During the Civil War, tin cans of Maine's wild blueberries were supplied to the Union troops to prevent scurvy (a disease caused by lack of vitamin C). After the war ended, people from many states had developed a taste for wild blueberries.

The industry grew when frozen food was invented in 1924. Later, researchers at the University of Maine found better ways to grow the plants. For example, after harvesting the berries, fields were burned so that new bushes would grow. Mowing replaced burning. It is cheaper and more environmentally friendly.

In 1991, the state legislature and governor declared the wild blueberry the official Maine berry. The industry grew considerably when researchers began reporting the health benefits of eating blueberries, starting in 1998. Today, Maine is the largest producer of wild blueberries in the world. The state produces 99 percent of the wild blueberries in the nation and 40 percent of the world's supply. In 2008, the economic value to Maine was about $75 million, and almost 90 million pounds (almost 41 million kilograms) of wild blueberries were grown.

electrical, and communications equipment is a steadily growing industry. Factories produce frozen vegetables and fruits, frozen and canned fish, and canned chowders and soups. Other factories pack blueberries, apples, and potatoes for shipping.

Boat and shipbuilding and repair continue to be important industries. Some shipbuilding companies make large seagoing ships. Other boatyards along the coast make small boats and yachts. Near Portland, Maine's largest city, factories manufacture aerospace equipment.

Once considered food for poor people, lobsters, such as these in Penobscot Bay, are an important industry today.

Fishing, Agriculture, and Mining

Fishing, agriculture, and mining make up about 3 percent of Maine's economy. Most harbors along Maine's coast and islands support fleets of fishing boats. They bring in ocean fish such as herring, cod, haddock, and flounder. Fish farms near the coast raise Atlantic salmon. Fisheries also catch lobsters, crabs, clams, and mussels. In 2008, more than 67 million pounds (30.5 million kg) of Maine lobsters, worth more than $235 million, were harvested. Other people employed in the industry clean, prepare, pack, and ship fish and shellfish.

Since 1820, potatoes have been Maine's main crop. The state is the number one potato producer in New England and one of the top producers in the nation. Most potato farms are in Aroostook County and the St. John River Valley. Some popular varieties of potato grown there include Kennebec, Green Mountain, Katahdin, and Carolla, among others. Other Maine crops include apples, oats, and hay. In New England, the state ranks second in the production of eggs and milk. Maine is the second largest producer of maple syrup in the nation.

Maine has a small mining industry. The major materials mined today are sand, gravel, crushed stone, granite, slate, and limestone. Tourmaline is the state's mineral and has been mined in Maine since the 1820s.

Service Industries

The largest part of Maine's economy is focused on services. Jobs in the services industry are in health care, finance, insurance, trade, information, government, and tourism. Maine is a national leader in health insurance coverage for its people. Government is a large employer in the state. Government services include the operation of public schools, hospitals, and military bases. Most government activities are based in Augusta, the state capital.

The state's natural beauty is important to its tourist industry. Tourism in Maine boomed after the Civil War. By steamboats and train, people from the East and Midwest came to vacation in Maine. Since the 1980s, tourism has grown considerably, especially in the coastal areas. Maine has more than 542,600 acres (2,196 sq km) of state and national parks. These include Acadia National Park, the second most visited national park in the United States. The state's rivers and lakes attract people who like to fish, boat, hike, and camp.

With 7 miles (about 11 km) of beautiful sandy beach, Old Orchard Beach in Saco Bay has been a favorite tourist spot for more than 170 years.

Tourists come in the fall and winter to hunt, ski, and snowmobile. Many tourists visit historical sites such as the sixty-five lighthouses along the coast. Tourism is one of the largest service industries in the state. Millions of tourists visit Maine every year and contribute more than $5 billion per year to the economy of the state.

Maine is expected to have slow, steady economic growth. The state's economic future includes its ports, which are important for transportation on the Atlantic coast to other ports worldwide. Currently, Portland is the largest port in New England in tonnage. Maine's service industry, including tourism, is expected to grow. Banks and insurance companies have been moving their headquarters to Maine. The state is developing other industries, such as technology, which includes software companies and Internet service providers.

Chapter 5

PEOPLE FROM MAINE:
PAST AND PRESENT

Many famous people in numerous fields of endeavor call Maine their home. They've influenced the state, the nation, and the world. The following are just a sample of Maine's notable celebrities.

Leon Lenwood (L. L.) Bean (1872–1967) In 1912, Bean invented a rubber and leather boot to keep his feet dry while hiking in the woods. His Maine Hunting Shoe and other outdoor products that he invented sold across the nation. In 1934, he founded L. L. Bean in Freeport, Maine, to sell quality outdoor products. Today, L. L. Bean products are sold worldwide, and the Freeport store is a popular stop for millions of tourists every year.

Milton Bradley (1836–1911) Born in Vienna, Maine, Bradley invented his first board game in 1860. A year later, his game had sold more than forty-five thousand copies and eventually was titled The Game of Life. With this success, he formed Milton Bradley and Company in 1864. His company created many new board games still popular today, including Yahtzee, Chutes and Ladders, and Candy Land. Bradley is credited with launching the game industry in North America.

Joshua L. Chamberlain (1828–1914) In 1862, Chamberlain was a lieutenant colonel for the 20th Maine Infantry Regiment during the Civil War. At the Battle of Gettysburg, he and his troops turned back Confederate attacks on Little Round Top, which became the turning point of this battle. Chamberlain received the Congressional Medal of Honor for his accomplishment. Later, he became Maine's governor for four terms.

Outdoorsman L. L. Bean, seen here testing wooden duck decoys, established a store and mail-order business in Freeport, Maine.

Patrick Dempsey (1966–) Dempsey began acting in 1985 and has since appeared in more than forty movies, including *Enchanted* (2007) and *Made of Honor* (2008). In 2005, the Maine native got the role of Dr. Derek Shepherd, a surgeon, on the popular TV show *Grey's Anatomy*.

Dorothea Dix (1802–1887) Born in Hampden, Maine, Dix began teaching at the age of fourteen at a girls' school in Worcester, Massachusetts. She opened her own school in

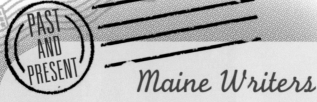

Maine Writers

Maine has been home to some of the greatest writers of yesterday and today. Stephen King, Henry Wadsworth Longfellow, and E. B. White are just a few of the notable authors and poets.

Stephen King (1947–) With the success of his first novel, *Carrie* (1974), King quit his teaching job and went on to write dozens of horror, fantasy, and suspense novels, short stories, and screenplays. A number of King's stories have been made into movies, including *Carrie* (1976), *The Shining* (1980), *Misery* (1990), *The Shawshank Redemption* (1995), and *The Green Mile* (1999). In 2003, he received the prestigious National Book Award.

Henry Wadsworth Longfellow (1807–1882) A native of Portland, Longfellow became the nation's best-known poet by the 1850s. By the time of his death, he was world famous. Longfellow was inspired by the history and beauty of Maine, which was reflected in many of his works. Three of his famous poems are "Evangeline" (1847), "The Song of Hiawatha" (1855), and "The Midnight Ride of Paul Revere" (1863).

Elwyn Brooks (E. B.) White (1899–1985) White began his writing career with the *New Yorker* magazine in 1925. He also wrote essays, poetry, and books. Many of his works tell about his life in Maine. White is the author of three beloved children's books: *Charlotte's Web* (1952), *Stuart Little* (1945), and *The Trumpet of the Swan* (1970).

Stephen King writes best-selling fiction from his home in Bangor, Maine.

Boston in 1821. Later, she became a nurse and devoted herself to the rights of the mentally ill. She worked tirelessly to improve the conditions and treatment in public institutions for the mentally ill in the United States, Canada, and Japan. During the Civil War, she served as the Union's superintendent of nurses.

William King (1768–1852) King campaigned vigorously in the early 1800s for Maine's independence from Massachusetts. In 1819, he was chosen as the president of Maine's constitutional convention. The next year, King won election as Maine's first governor. He continued his career in public service at both the federal and state levels.

Edmund Muskie (1914–1996) Muskie was the governor of Maine from 1955 to 1959. Elected to the U.S. Senate in 1959, he served as Maine's senator until 1981. During his time as governor and senator, he focused on the environment and worked on laws for clean air and water. From 1980 to 1981, Muskie was the U.S. secretary of state.

Tim Sample (1951–) Born in Boothbay, Maine, Sample was a correspondent for CBS news and regularly contributed to *CBS News Sunday Morning*. His segment on *Sunday Morning*, called "Postcards from Maine," is broadcast monthly.

Joan Benoit Samuelson (1957–) Samuelson was born in Cape Elizabeth, Maine. After breaking her leg while skiing, she took up running. The long-distance runner won the

Long-distance runner Joan Benoit Samuelson wins the women's marathon at the 1984 Olympics. In 1998, she established a new road race in Maine called the Peoples Heritage Beach to Beacon 10k.

Boston Marathon in 1979 and 1983. Making history in Los Angeles, California, she won the first-ever women's Olympic marathon at the 1984 Summer Games and clocked the second fastest time posted by a woman in a marathon.

Margaret Chase Smith (1897–1995) A popular public official, Smith became the first woman elected to both houses of the U.S. Congress. Smith served in the House of Representatives from 1940 to 1949 and in the Senate from 1949 to 1973. In 1989, President George H. W. Bush awarded Smith the Presidential Medal of Freedom, the nation's highest civilian honor.

Samantha Smith (1972–1985) In 1982, when Smith was ten years old, she wrote a letter to former Soviet Union president Yuri Andropov. She told him that she feared the Soviet Union and the United States would have a nuclear war. She ended by asking for peace. The next year, Andropov invited Smith to visit the USSR. Her trip made news worldwide and helped bring the two countries closer. Smith became America's youngest ambassador.

Louis Sockalexis (1871–1913) A Penobscot Indian from Indian Island, Maine, Sockalexis was the first Native American to play Major League Baseball, as well as the first minority player in the National League. Also called the Deerfoot of the Diamond, Sockalexis was an outfielder for the Cleveland Spiders. In 1915, the Cleveland team changed its name to the Cleveland Indians in memory of Sockalexis.

Percy Lebaron Spencer (1894–1970) Engineer Percy Spencer was working with radar at the Raytheon Company when he noticed a melting candy bar in his pocket. This accident led him to create a device that cooked food using microwave radiation. The first microwave was called Radarange. Built in 1947, it was about 6 feet tall (1.8 m) and weighed 750 pounds (340 kg). Spencer's work with microwaves also resulted in significant advances in radar.

Robert Stanley (1954–) Born in Portland, Stanley was a Major League Baseball pitcher. He pitched for the Boston Red Sox from 1977 through 1989. Stanley was an All-Star in 1979 and 1983 and pitched in the 1986 World Series.

Timeline

9500 BCE Ancestors of Native Americans arrive.

1498 John Cabot explores the Maine coast.

1607 English settlers establish Popham Colony near Kennebec River.

1623 First sawmill in the nation begins operation.

1641 Gorgeana (now York) becomes the first English city in America.

1677 Massachusetts gains title to Maine.

1775 The first naval battle of the Revolutionary War occurs off the Maine coast.

1819 Maine prepares for statehood by writing its first constitution.

1820 Maine becomes the twenty-third state.

1842 The Webster-Ashburton Treaty establishes the Maine-Canada border.

1861–1865 Maine sides with the Union during the American Civil War.

1909 A new state flag is created and approved by the Maine legislature.

1950s–1960s New industries arrive, like food packaging and electronics manufacturing.

1980s Tourism industry has significant growth.

2000 Maine legislature is the first in the nation to pass a bill lowering the costs of prescription drugs for residents.

2004 Maine Rx Plus allows discount prices for prescription drugs.

2005 Maine is the first state to begin a health insurance program, called Dirigo Health, for all residents.

2009 Maine is ranked first of all fifty U.S. states for the electronic delivery of public service and citizen participation in governance.

2010 The federal government ranks Maine as a top-ten state for keeping unhealthy foods out of schools.

State motto:	*Dirigo* ("I Lead")
State capital:	Augusta
State flag:	Maine's state flag, adopted in 1909, has the state seal on a blue background.
State seal:	The state seal, adopted in 1820, shows a farmer with a scythe that represents agriculture. A seaman leaning on an anchor stands for fishing. These figures support a shield that displays a pine tree, moose, land, and water. The pine represents Maine's forests, and the moose symbolizes the state's undisturbed wildlife areas. At the top, the North Star represents Maine's northern location.
State flower:	White pinecone and tassel
State bird:	Chickadee
State tree:	White pine
State fruit:	Wild blueberry
Statehood date and number:	March 15, 1820; the twenty-third state
State nickname:	Pine Tree State
Total area and U.S. rank:	35,385 square miles (91,647 square km); thirty-ninth largest state

State flag

State seal

Population:	1,316,456
Highest elevation:	Mount Katahdin, 5,267 feet (1,606 m) above sea level
Lowest elevation:	Sea level, where Maine meets the Atlantic Ocean in the east
Major rivers:	Androscoggin River, Saco River, St. Croix River, St. John River
Major lakes:	Moosehead Lake, Belgrade Lakes, Grand Lake, Rangeley Lake, Sebago Lake
Hottest recorded temperature:	105°F (41°C) at North Bridgton on July 10, 1911;
Coldest recorded temperature:	–48°F (–44°C) at Van Buren on January 19, 1925
Origin of state name:	Named by French explorers after the region of Maine in France
Chief agricultural products:	Wild blueberries, potatoes, eggs, milk
Major industries:	Services, tourism, forestry, fishing, fruit farming, dairy farming

Chickadee

White pinecone and tassel

automation Work done by computers and machines.

bay A part of a sea or lake that cuts into the shoreline.

biotechnology The use of biological processes, organisms, or systems to manufacture products.

constitution A written document that sets up the principles and laws for a state or country's government.

cove A small, sheltered inlet in the shoreline of a sea, river, or lake.

free state A state without slaves.

gross domestic product (GDP) The total value of all goods and services produced in a state or country.

harbor A sheltered part of a body of water deep enough for ships to anchor.

hydroelectric power Energy that is generated by flowing water.

legislature A group of elected individuals who make and change laws.

logger A person or company in the business of harvesting trees for wood.

manufacture To produce or assemble.

patriot A person who supports his or her country.

plantation A unit of local government in Maine. A plantation has a limited form of self-government.

plateau An area of high ground with a level top.

pulp Wood that is ground up to make paper products.

salt marsh Low-lying wet land that is often flooded with salt water.

textile Woven fabric.

tourmaline A gemstone that exists in many colors.

town meeting An annual meeting in which residents can take a direct part in their local government.

tree farm An area where trees are grown commercially for their wood products.

FOR MORE INFORMATION

Environment Maine

39 Exchange Street #301

Portland, ME 04101

(207) 253-1965

Web site: http://www.environmentmaine.org

Environment Maine is a statewide, citizen-based organization that advocates for Maine's environment.

Maine Better Transportation Association

146 State Street

Augusta, ME 04330

(207) 622-0526

Web site: http://www.mbtaonline.org

Since 1939, the Maine Better Transportation Association has been advocating for safe, efficient transportation networks for roads, bridges, airports, ports, and trains.

Maine Coast Heritage Trust

1 Bowdoin Mill Island, Suite 201

Topsham, ME 04086

(207) 729-7366

Web site: http://www.mcht.org

Founded in 1970, the Maine Coast Heritage Trust conserves and stewards Maine's coastal lands and islands and promotes the conservation of natural places.

Maine Department of Marine Resources

21 State House Station

Augusta, ME 04333-0021

(207) 624-6550

Web site: http://www.maine.gov/dmr

This department conserves and develops marine resources, conducts scientific research, and promotes and develops the Maine coastal fishing industries. The department also works with government officials concerning activities on coastal waters.

Maine Development Foundation

295 Water Street, Suite 5

Augusta, ME 04330

(207) 622-6345

Web site: http://www.mdf.org

The Maine Development Foundation drives economic growth for Maine through its programs and research.

Maine Folklife Center

5773 South Stevens, Room 112B

Orono, ME 04469-5773

(207) 581-1891

Web site: http://www.umaine.edu/folklife

The Maine Folklife Center collects, interprets, and preserves Maine's cultural heritage.

Maine Historical Society

Maine Historical Society

489 Congress Street

Portland, ME 04101

(207) 774–1822

Web site: http://www.mainehistory.org

Established in 1822, the society seeks to foster a deeper understanding of and appreciation for Maine history through programs and publications.

Maine Maritime Museum

243 Washington Street

Bath, ME 04530

(207) 443-1316

Web site: http://www.mainemaritimemuseum.org

The Maine Maritime Museum offers many opportunities to explore Maine's maritime heritage and culture.

Maine State Library

64 State House Station

Augusta, ME 04333-0064

(207) 287-5600

Web site: http://www.maine.gov/msl/index.shtml

The Maine State Library provides access to information and library services and has extensive information resources about the state.

Marine Environmental Research Institute

55 Main Street

Blue Hill, ME 04614

(207) 374-2135

Web site: http://www.meriresearch.org

Since 1990, the Marine Environmental Research Institute has worked to protect the health and biodiversity of the marine environment.

Web Sites

Due to the changing nature of Internet links, Rosen Publishing has developed an online list of Web sites related to the subject of this book. This site is updated regularly. Please use this link to access the list:

http://www.rosenlinks.com/uspp/mepp

FOR FURTHER READING

Brown, Jonatha. *Maine* (Portraits of the States). New York, NY: Gareth Stevens Publishing, 2007.

Carlton, Susan. *Lobsterland*. New York, NY: Henry Holt, 2007.

Cronin, Stephen. *The Island: A Young Boy's Journey to Manhood on Matinicus Island*. Lincoln, NE: iUniverse, Inc., 2007.

DeFord, Deborah H. *Maine. The Pine Tree State*. Milwaukee, WI: World Almanac Library, 2003.

Dornfeld, Margaret, and Joyce Hart. *Maine* (Celebrate the States). Tarrytown, NY: Marshall Cavendish Children's Books, 2010.

Heinrichs, Ann. *Maine*. New York, NY: Children's Press, 2008.

Hicks, Terry Allan. *Maine*. New York, NY: Marshall Cavendish Benchmark, 2006.

House, Katherine L. *Lighthouses for Kids: History, Science, and Lore with 21 Activities*. Chicago, IL: Chicago Review Press, 2008.

Jones, Kimberly K. *Sand Dollar Summer*. New York, NY: Margaret K. McElderry, 2006.

Kidwell, Al. *Coastal Birds: A Guide to Birds of Maine's Beautiful Coastline*. Yarmouth, MD: Delorme, 2003.

Kress, Stephen W. *Project Puffin: How We Brought Puffins Back to Egg Rock*. Gardiner, ME: Tilbury House Publishers, 1999.

Philips, Dave. *Seeds of a Nation: Maine*. San Diego, CA: KidHaven Press, 2004.

Sample, Tim, and Steve D. Bither. *Maine Curiosities: Quirky Characters, Roadside Oddities, and Other Offbeat Stuff*. Guilford, CT: Globe Pequot, 2006.

Schmidt, Gary D. *Lizzie Bright and the Buckminster Boy*. New York, NY: Clarion Books, 2004.

Speare, Elizabeth George. *The Sign of the Beaver*. Boston, MA: Houghton Mifflin Books for Children, 1983.

Webster, Christine. *Maine*. New York, NY: Children's Press, 2003.

Zschock, Martha. *Hello, Maine!* Beverly, MA: Commonwealth Editions, 2010.

BIBLIOGRAPHY

Bell, Daniel J., Lisa J. Rowland, John Smagula, and Frank Drummond. "Recent Advances in the Biology and Genetics of Lowbush Blueberry." University of Maine, October 2009. Retrieved November 12, 2009 (http://www.umaine.edu/mafes/elec_pubs/techbulletins/tb203.pdf).

Colgan, Charles S. "Maine's Technology Sectors and Clusters: Status and Strategy." MaineInnovation.com, March 2008. Retrieved November 11, 2009 (http://www.maineinnovation.com/mie/pdfs/Cluster_Report_Executive_Summary_FINAL_041508.pdf).

Graham, Frank. "The Puffin Man." *Audubon*, December 2003. Retrieved November 2, 2009 (http://www.audubonmagazine.org/profile/profile0312.html).

Maine Department of Natural Resources. "Historical Maine Lobster Landings." 2008. Retrieved November 6, 2009 (http://www.maine.gov/dmr/commercialfishing/historicaldata.htm).

Maine Municipal Association. "Local Government in Maine." 2008. Retrieved November 4, 2009 (http://www.memun.org/public/local_govt/default.htm).

Maine Pulp and Paper Association. "A Brief History of Papermaking in Maine." 2004. Retrieved November 8, 2009 (http://www.pulpandpaper.org/html/history_of_papermaking.html).

McNair, Wesley, ed. *A Place Called Maine: Twenty-Four Authors on the Maine Experience*. Rockport, ME: Down East Books, 2008.

National Audubon Society. "26 Questions About Puffins." 2009. Retrieved November 2, 2009 (http://www.audubon.org/BIRD/PUFFIN/PuffinQuestions.html).

Seymour, Tom. *Tom Seymour's Maine: A Maine Anthology*. Lincoln, NE: iUniverse, Inc., 2003.

Seymour, Tom, and Wayne Curtis. *Maine Off the Beaten Path*. Springfield, TN: GPP Travel, 2008.

State of Maine. "Facts About Maine." 2009. Retrieved October 29, 2009 (http://www.maine.gov/portal/facts_history/facts.html).

State of Maine. "Maine Court History." 2008. Retrieved November 4, 2009 (http://www.courts.state.me.us/maine_courts/education/history.shtml).

Stover, Arthur Douglas. *Eminent Mainers: Succinct Biographies of Thousands of Amazing Mainers, Mostly Dead, and a Few People from Away Who Have Done Something Useful Within the State of Maine*. Gardiner, ME: Tilbury House Publishers, 2006.

Tree, Christina, and Nancy English. *Maine: An Explorer's Guide*. Woodstock, VT: The Countryman Press, 2008.

U.S. Census Bureau. "State and County Quick Facts: Maine." September 4, 2009. Retrieved November 1, 2009 (http://quickfacts.census.gov/qfd/states/23000.html).

U.S. Department of Labor. "Economy at a Glance: Maine." 2009. Retrieved November 8, 2009 (http://www.bls.gov/eag/eag.me.htm).

Woodard, Colin. *The Lobster Coast: Rebels, Rusticators, and the Struggle for a Forgotten Frontier*. New York, NY: Penguin, 2005.

Yarborough, David E. "The Wild Blueberry in Maine." March 2003. Retrieved November 12, 2009 (http://www.wildblueberries.maine.edu/PDF/wildblueberryinME.pdf).

INDEX

A

Acadia National Park, 6, 28
Andropov, Yuri, 35
Augusta, 15, 19, 20, 28

B

Bean, L. L., 30
Bradley, Milton, 30
Bush, George H. W., 35

C

Chamberlain, Joshua L., 31
Civil War, 14, 15–16, 24, 26, 28, 31, 33
constitutional conventions, 18, 33
Court Reorganization Act of 1852, 22

D

Dempsey, Patrick, 31
Dix, Dorothea, 31, 33

G

Gulf of Maine, 8

H

Hamlin, Hannibal, 16

K

King, Stephen, 32
King, William, 33
Kress, Stephen W., 8

L

lighthouses, 5, 29
Lincoln, Abraham, 16
Longfellow, Henry Wadsworth, 32

M

Maine
  economy of, 5, 16–17, 24–29
  geography of, 5, 6–11, 16–17
  government of, 13, 16, 17, 18–23, 26, 31, 33
  history of, 5, 8, 12–17, 22, 26, 28
  people from, 30–36
Muskie, Edmund, 33

O

Old Orchard Beach, 9

P

Portland, 7, 9, 15, 27, 29, 32, 36
Project Puffin, 8

R

Revolutionary War, 15

S

Sample, Tim, 33
Samuelson, Joan Benoit, 33, 35
Smith, Margaret Chase, 35
Smith, Samantha, 35
Sockalexis, Louis, 35
Spencer, Percy Lebaron, 36
Stanley, Robert, 36

T

town meetings, 21

U

University of Maine, 26

W

White, E. B., 32
wild blueberries, 5, 10, 26, 27

About the Author

Judy Monroe Peterson holds two master's degrees and is the author of numerous educational books for young people. She is a former technical, health care, and academic librarian and college faculty member; a research scientist; and curriculum editor with more than twenty-five years of experience. She has taught courses at 3M, the University of Minnesota, and Lake Superior College. Currently, she is a writer and editor of K–12 and post–high school curriculum materials on a variety of subjects, including social studies, history, and government.

Photo Credits

Cover (top left) Lass/Getty Images; cover (top right), pp. 11, 17, 23, 25, 29 © AP Images; cover (bottom) Ron and Patty Thomas/Getty Images; pp. 3, 6, 12, 18, 24, 30, 37 © www.istockphoto.com; p. 4 © GeoAtlas; p. 7 © www.istockphotocom/Kenneth C. Zirkel; p. 9 © www.istockphoto.com.com/Michael Czosnek; p. 13 © Bristol City Museum and Art Gallery, UK/The Bridgeman Art Library; p. 16 George Eastman House/Getty Images; p. 19 © age fotostock/Superstock; p. 20 © www.istockphoto.com/Chee-Onn Leong; p. 27 © IndexStock/Superstock; p. 31 GeorgeStrock/Time Life Pictures/Getty Images; p. 32 Bennett Raglin/WireImage/Getty Images; p. 34 Tony Duffy/Getty Images; p. 38 (left) Courtesy of Robesus, Inc.; p. 39 (left) © www.istockphoto.com com/Frank Leung; p. 39 (right) © Ned Therrien/Visuals Unlimited.

Designer: Les Kanturek; Editor: Kathy Kuhtz Campbell
Photo Researcher: Marty Levick